Hamsters 101

The Complete Beginner's Guide

Smart, Simple Care for Raising a Happy, Healthy Hamster

By **Evan Hartley**

Book 1 of The Happy Hamster Series

CreatureWise Publishing

Disclaimer

This book is here to guide and support you, but it isn't a replacement for professional veterinary care. Every hamster is unique, and if you ever have concerns about your pet's health, always reach out to a qualified exotic animal veterinarian for advice that's tailored to your little one.

Dedication Page

For every first-time hamster owner

who wants to do things right from the start.

Before You Begin

You may notice that certain ideas or tips show up more than once throughout this book. That's on purpose. Hamster care can feel overwhelming for first-time owners, and some lessons are worth repeating in different contexts to help them really stick.

The goal isn't to fill pages — it's to make sure you feel confident and supported every step of the way.

TABLE OF CONTENTS

Introduction

So, you're thinking about getting a hamster — or maybe you already have one, and now you're wondering what exactly you signed up for. Either way, welcome. You've just taken the first step toward becoming the kind of hamster owner every little fluffball deserves.

This book isn't full of fluffy generalities, misleading advice from pet store employees, or copy-pasted facts from the internet. It's a straight-talking, science-backed, hands-on guide written for real people with real lives — people who want to do right by their hamster without buying ten kinds of bedding or memorizing Latin species names.

You'll learn how to choose the right hamster, set up a safe and enriching home, feed it well, bond with it without stress, and recognize signs of illness early. And when the time comes to say goodbye, this book will help you handle it with compassion and honesty.

No jargon. No lectures. Just the kind of practical advice you wish came stapled to the hamster cage.

Let's get into it.

1

Meet the Hamster – Breeds & Personalities

So, you've decided to get a hamster. Or maybe you're still thinking about it but you've already googled things like "do hamsters smell," "are hamsters hard to take care of," or "why is that hamster staring at me like it knows things." Either way—good news: you're in the right place.

Before you dive into hamster parenthood, you need to understand one important truth:

Not all hamsters are created equal.

They may all fit in your palm, but they don't all fit into the same lifestyle. Some are friendly and slow-moving. Others are tiny, lightning-fast, and about as snuggly as a marble in a sock.

This chapter is your full rundown of who's who in the hamster world—so you don't end up with a high-speed escape artist when you wanted a cuddly couch potato.

The 5 Hamsters You'll Actually See in Pet Stores

There are around 20 species of wild hamsters out there, but only **five** are commonly kept as pets. If you walk into a pet store or look up reputable breeders, you'll likely meet one of these five:

1. Syrian Hamster

Also known as: Golden Hamster, Teddy Bear Hamster, Fancy Hamster

- **Size:** 5–7 inches (the biggest of the bunch)
- **Personality:** Calm, slow-moving, and relatively easy to tame
- **Best For:** First-time owners, kids (with supervision), adults who want a single, handleable pet
- **Solo or Social?:** Must be kept alone. No exceptions.

Syrian hamsters are the classic "starter hamster"—but don't let that make them sound boring. They're full of charm and tend to bond well with patient owners. They're also strictly solitary, so if you're tempted to get two "to keep each other company," don't. You'll just end up needing a second cage—and possibly a vet.

2. Roborovski Hamster

Also known as: Robo Hamster, Blink-and-it's-Gone

- **Size:** About 2 inches (tiny!)
- **Personality:** Extremely fast, easily startled, not cuddly
- **Best For:** Observers, not handlers. Good for watching, not for holding.
- **Solo or Social?:** Can live in pairs if raised together, but it's tricky.

Robos are the smallest and fastest hamster species. They're cute, active, and fun to watch—but forget about holding one. They can vanish between your fingers like magic, and chasing them around the living room isn't anyone's idea of bonding.

3. Campbell's Dwarf Hamster

Also known as: Russian Dwarf Hamster (not to be confused with Winter White)

- **Size:** About 4 inches

- **Personality:** Curious, energetic, can be nippy if not handled gently

- **Best For:** Adults or older kids with quick hands and some patience

- **Solo or Social?:** Can live in same-sex pairs or small groups, but monitor closely

Campbell's hamsters are small, sassy, and full of attitude. They're entertaining, but they don't always enjoy being picked up. You'll need to earn their trust slowly—and even then, expect them to stay a little independent.

4. Winter White Dwarf Hamster

Also known as: Djungarian Hamster, Chubby Marshmallow

- **Size:** 3.5–4 inches

- **Personality:** Gentle, calm, more tolerant of handling than other dwarfs

- **Best For:** Calm households, first-timers who want a dwarf hamster

- **Solo or Social?:** Can sometimes live with same-species siblings if introduced young

Winter Whites are a little rounder and a little calmer than Campbell's. They're known for their sweet nature—and yes, their fur can turn white in winter if they're exposed to a natural light cycle (though most indoor lighting prevents that). Think of them as the soft-spoken cousin at the hamster family reunion.

5. Chinese Hamster

Also known as: Tail Hamster, Ninja Mouse

- **Size:** Around 4 inches, with a long tail

- **Personality:** Quiet, agile, gentle, likes to perch in your hand

- **Best For:** Adults who want a more unique, mellow hamster

- **Solo or Social?:** Best kept alone

Chinese hamsters aren't technically "true" hamsters, but they're legal to own and care for like the others. They've got a longer tail, a longer body, and a chill personality that's perfect for someone who doesn't need a high-maintenance pet.

Hamster Matchmaking: Which One Should You Get?

There's no one-size-fits-all hamster. Use this simple chart to get a rough idea of which one might fit your life:

Your Priority	Best Match
Easy to hold, beginner-friendly	Syrian
Fun to watch, low handling	Roborovski
Small but spunky	Campbell's
Soft, calm, and tameable	Winter White
Unique, mellow, and agile	Chinese

A Word on Hybrids

Some pet stores—especially chain stores—sell dwarf hamsters without clearly identifying the species. Often, these are **hybrids** between Campbell's and Winter Whites. While they can be cute, hybrids are more prone to health issues (especially diabetes), unpredictable behavior, and aggression.

If possible, get your hamster from a **reputable breeder or rescue** that can confirm the species. It'll save you a lot of guesswork—and vet bills—later on.

One Hamster, One Home

Let's clear up one of the biggest misunderstandings in hamster care:

Most hamsters are solitary.

This means:

- Syrians must be housed alone. No exceptions.

- Chinese should also live solo.

- Robos, Campbell's, and Winter Whites *may* cohabit under the right conditions—but even then, things can go wrong quickly.

Fighting, injury, even death—it's not worth the risk unless you're very experienced and have a backup cage ready to go.

Golden rule: If in doubt, house your hamster alone. They won't get lonely, but they might get eaten if you try to force a roommate.

Summary: Know Who You're Getting

Before you bring a hamster home, ask yourself:

- Do I want a pet I can hold, or just one to observe?

- Can I handle a fast-moving animal, or do I need something slower?

- Am I okay with just one, or am I trying to house more than one?

Choosing the right species upfront makes everything else—taming, bonding, feeding, cage setup—a lot easier.

Next up, we'll build your hamster's dream home.

2

Hamster Housing 101 – Cages That Don't Suck

Let's get something out of the way up front:

Most hamster cages sold in pet stores are too small, too cheap, and too dangerous. Yes, even the ones with fancy packaging and photos of smiling children.

If you want your hamster to live a long, healthy, and happy life, you need to ignore the advertising and understand what actually matters when it comes to housing. In this chapter, we'll walk through everything you need to know to choose the right cage — no guesswork, no gimmicks.

The Truth About Cage Size

If a cage can fit on a dinner plate, it's not big enough. Period.

Minimum size (based on real research, not marketing):

- **Floor space:** At least **600 square inches** (That's about **30" x 20"** of uninterrupted floor — not counting multiple levels or tubes.)

- **Height:** Not too tall. Hamsters aren't squirrels. If they fall, they can get seriously hurt.

Many countries have minimum standards for hamster cages. In the U.S., there's no law, so pet stores get away with selling cages that are far too small. That's why owners often report bar-chewing, stress, aggression, or escape attempts. It's not "bad behavior" — it's a bored, anxious animal trapped in a shoebox.

Good Cage Types (And Why They Work)

Let's talk about what *does* work.

1. Glass Tanks (Aquariums)

- **Pros:** Solid sides, no bar chewing, holds deep bedding

- **Cons:** Heavy, poor ventilation if not properly modified

- **Best for:** Hamsters who kick bedding everywhere

If you go this route, make sure to use a **mesh lid** for airflow, and keep it in a cool room. A 40-gallon breeder tank is ideal.

2. Bin Cages (DIY Plastic Storage Bins)

- **Pros:** Cheap, customizable, safe, surprisingly spacious

- **Cons:** Requires tools to make (drilling, cutting)

- **Best for:** Budget-friendly, hands-on owners

A 50 –100 quart bin with a ventilated lid and side panels can be turned into a hamster mansion for under $40. Just make sure to smooth any cut edges.

3. IKEA Detolf (Converted Glass Cabinet)

- **Pros:** Huge floor space, stylish, popular among hobbyists

- **Cons:** Requires DIY mods, must be placed on its side

- **Best for:** Dedicated owners who want the hamster version of a penthouse

Hamster lovers love this one for a reason — it's beautiful and functional, once set up right.

Cage Types to Avoid (Seriously, Don't Do It)

Wire cages with tiny platforms

Usually sold as "starter kits," these are too small, too open, and designed more for marketing than actual care. Hamsters can squeeze through gaps, get limbs stuck, or fall from unsafe heights.

Tubes and modular cage systems

They look fun. They are not. Tubes are hard to clean, low on airflow, and easy to get stuck in. Also: hamsters pee in them, then sleep in them, then get sick.

Cages with built-in wheels or plastic levels

Wheels are often too small (more on that in Chapter 3), and the ramps can be dangerous. A proper cage should be a blank canvas — not a plastic playground designed by someone who's never owned a rodent.

Bar Spacing and Escape Risks

If you choose a wire cage (and it's big enough), make sure the **bar spacing is no wider than 1/4 inch** (0.6 cm). Dwarf hamsters can squeeze through shockingly small spaces — if they can fit their head, they can squeeze the rest through.

For Syrians, 1/2 inch (1.2 cm) spacing is okay — but still check for escape points around doors and latches.

Ventilation & Location

Where you place the cage matters too.

- Keep it in a **quiet room**, away from direct sun, drafts, and loud noise.

- Don't put it on the floor — raise it slightly so vibrations from walking don't stress the hamster.

- Avoid kitchens, bathrooms, and laundry rooms — they're noisy, smelly, and humid.

Good airflow is important, especially in glass or plastic setups. Without it, ammonia from urine builds up, causing respiratory problems.

Security & Lids

Hamsters are excellent climbers. Many have escaped through **loose lids** or **improperly latched cage doors**.

- If your cage has a lid — weigh it down or clip it shut.

- If it has doors — test the locks. Can you open them easily with one finger? So can your hamster.

You don't want to wake up and find your hamster decided to remodel your sock drawer.

Don't Trust the Box — Trust the Ruler

Cages will often say "suitable for hamsters" right on the label. They're lying.

Instead of trusting labels, **measure the floor space** yourself:

Length × Width = Square Inches of Usable Floor

(Exclude levels, ramps, and accessories.)

You want **at least 600 square inches** More is better. Always.

Summary: What Makes a Good Cage?

- 600+ sq. inches of **unbroken floor space**

- Solid, escape-proof build

- Safe materials (no sharp plastic, no zinc-coated bars)

- Good airflow

- Space for **deep bedding**, hideouts, wheel, food, and toys

- Easy to clean and maintain

3

Interior Design for Hamsters – Bedding, Wheels, Hides & Essentials

Your hamster's cage is now ready. Big, safe, and empty. Now what?

This is where most new owners either:

1. Dump in some colorful fluff and a plastic igloo…

2. Or go broke buying every shiny product in the hamster aisle.

Let's avoid both.

This chapter will show you what actually belongs inside your hamster's cage — and what's just overpriced junk. No fluff (unless it's paper-based). No gimmicks. Just the good stuff.

First Things First: What Does a Hamster *Really* Need?

Let's break it down. Your hamster's cage needs to include:

- Bedding (deep and diggable)
- A proper wheel
- A hideout (or two)
- Food bowl (optional)
- Water bottle or dish
- Sand bath

- Toys for chewing and enrichment

That's it. Everything else is just interior decoration.

Bedding: Deep, Not Decorative

Bedding is where your hamster eats, sleeps, pees, burrows, and builds its little underground empire. The deeper, the better.

What to Look For:

- **Soft but firm** (holds shape for burrows)

- **Unscented** (no perfumes or additives)

- **Dust-free** (respiratory safety)

- **Absorbent** (controls odor, moisture)

Recommended Bedding Materials:

- **Paper-based bedding** (like Carefresh or Kaytee Clean & Cozy)

- **Aspen shavings** (safe wood, but less cozy)

- **Hemp bedding** (low-dust, eco-friendly)

Bedding to Avoid:

- Pine or cedar (toxic oils)

- Fluffy cotton or "hamster wool" (choking hazard)

- Scented bedding (can cause allergies, sneezing, eye issues)

How Deep Should It Be?

At least **6 inches deep**, ideally 10–12 inches for Syrians. Dwarf hamsters love to burrow too, but even they get stuck with just a thin layer in most cages.

Give them room to dig — they'll do the decorating for you.

The Wheel: No, That Tiny One Is Not Okay

If you bought a cage that came with a wheel — throw it out. Chances are, it's too small, too stiff, or just plain dangerous.

A Good Wheel Must Be:

- **Large enough** so the hamster doesn't arch its back
- **Silent** (or close to it)
- **Solid-surface** (no wire bars — those cause injury)

Minimum Size Guidelines:

- **Syrian hamsters:** At least **11–12 inches** in diameter
- **Dwarf hamsters:** At least **8 inches**

Barred or mesh wheels can lead to foot injuries (called bumblefoot), broken toes, or worse. Solid plastic or cork-lined wheels are ideal. Bonus if they're easy to remove and clean.

Hideouts: The Bedroom Your Hamster Actually Wants

Every hamster needs at least one **hideout** — a cozy, dark place to sleep and feel safe.

Must-Haves:

- **No plastic** — hamsters chew everything

- **Dark inside** — let them feel secure

- **Big enough to turn around** comfortably

- **Ventilated** — no moisture traps

Best Options:

- Wooden houses

- Cork tunnels

- Terracotta pots

- DIY cardboard boxes

Tip: Put a large handful of clean, unscented **nesting paper** nearby and let them drag it into the hide themselves. It's part of the fun.

Food & Water: Bowl or Scatter?

You'll need either a food bowl or scatter feeding — both work.

- **Bowl feeding:** Keeps track of how much they're eating.

- **Scatter feeding:** Encourages foraging and natural behaviors.

Some owners do both. Use **ceramic bowls** (heavy and chew-proof) and avoid plastic.

For water, a standard **water bottle** with a metal spout is best — but **some hamsters prefer a shallow ceramic dish.** Try both and see what your hamster likes.

Sand Baths: Not Optional

Despite what the name suggests, hamsters don't bathe in water. They roll in sand to stay clean and oil-free.

What You Need:

- A container at least 2x the size of your hamster
- 1–2 inches of **dust-free, fine sand**

Approved Sands:

- **Chinchilla bathing sand** (not dust!)
- **Children's play sand** (baked to remove moisture)
- **Reptile sand** (as long as it's additive-free)

Avoid scented sand, glitter sand, or anything labeled "dust" — that's a lung problem waiting to happen.

Toys & Enrichment

You don't need a toy aisle explosion — but your hamster does need things to **chew, climb, and explore**.

Great Additions:

- Wooden chew sticks
- Cardboard tubes
- Cork logs
- Foraging toys
- Paper towel rolls
- Hanging bridges or platforms

Rotate toys weekly to keep things fresh. Think less "hamster playground" and more "natural jungle gym."

What NOT to Put in the Cage

Let's save you some money and your hamster some misery.

- Cotton nest fluff

- Plastic igloos

- Ladders with gaps

- Hanging wire levels

- Metal food dishes (they tip, rust, or get chewed)

- Exercise balls (outside the cage AND inside — we'll get into that later)

Putting It All Together: The Setup

Here's a sample layout for a basic Syrian cage:

- **Left side:** Deep bedding and burrow zone

- **Back corner:** Wooden hideout, nesting area

- **Center:** Large wheel, on a flat surface

- **Right side:** Sand bath in a ceramic dish

- **Front corner:** Food bowl and water bottle

- **Scattered:** Toys, chew sticks, platforms

Dwarf hamster layout? Same idea, just smaller scale — but still plenty of space and deep bedding.

Summary: The Essentials Checklist

- 600+ sq in cage
- 6–12 inches of safe, unscented bedding
- Properly sized, solid-surface wheel
- Hideout (wood, cardboard, or ceramic)
- Water bottle or dish
- Food bowl or scatter area
- Sand bath with safe sand
- Chew toys & foraging activities
- Room to dig, burrow, explore

4

Feeding Your Hamster – What Helps, What Harms

You'd think feeding a hamster would be simple: just toss in a few pellets, maybe a carrot stick, and you're done, right?

Not quite.

Hamsters may be tiny, but their nutritional needs are surprisingly specific. The wrong food can cause obesity, diabetes, tooth problems, or even shorten their lifespan. The good news? Feeding them properly isn't hard — once you know what to look for (and what to avoid).

This chapter will break down exactly what your hamster should eat, how much, how often, and what's secretly turning your "healthy treat" into a sugar bomb.

The Basics: What Do Hamsters Eat?

Hamsters are **omnivores** — meaning they eat plants *and* animal-based proteins.

A healthy diet includes:

- A **high-quality pellet or seed mix** (the foundation)
- Small amounts of **fresh vegetables** and herbs
- Occasional **protein treats** (like mealworms or boiled egg)
- Fresh water — always available
- The **occasional fruit or safe treat** — *very occasional*

Think of their diet like a food pyramid. The base is a balanced dry mix. Fresh veg and proteins sit above that. Treats? Way up at the top — tiny amounts only.

Choosing a Commercial Food Mix (Without Getting Scammed)

This is where most people get it wrong.

Those colorful bags in the pet store with happy cartoon hamsters on them? A lot of them are **junk food in disguise**. Too much corn, too many colorful bits, sugary yogurt drops — it's hamster candy.

What to Look For:

- Protein content: **17–19%**

- Fat content: **4–7%**

- Fiber: **6–12%**

- **No added sugar, honey, or artificial colors**

Look for words like:

- "Complete diet"

- "Species-appropriate"

- "Fortified with vitamins and minerals"

And avoid vague labels like:

- "For small animals" (that includes rabbits and guinea pigs — totally different needs)

- "With fruity flavors!" (hamsters don't need strawberry puffs)

Seed Mix vs. Pellets: Which Is Better?

- **Pellets (lab blocks):**
  - ✓ Balanced nutrition in every bite
  - ✗ Boring; no foraging; some hamsters won't eat them
- **Seed Mixes:**
  - ✓ Encourages natural foraging behavior
  - ✗ Hamsters may pick out favorite bits and leave the healthy ones

Many experienced owners use **a mix of both**: a high-quality seed mix *and* a few pellets to ensure nutritional balance. Watch how your hamster eats and adjust as needed.

Fresh Veggies: The Good Stuff (in the Right Amount)

Hamsters love fresh food — but too much can cause diarrhea or bloating. Start small, just a bite-sized piece per day.

Safe Veggies (Offer Often):

- Broccoli
- Carrot (small amounts — high in sugar)
- Cucumber
- Zucchini
- Bell pepper (no seeds)
- Spinach (a few leaves)
- Romaine lettuce (not iceberg)

Use Sparingly:

- Kale

- Cauliflower

- Celery

- Beetroot

- Sweet corn (tiny amounts)

Always wash vegetables and serve **raw, plain, and at room temperature**. Remove uneaten fresh food after a few hours.

Fruits: Nature's Candy (Use Rarely)

Fruits are sweet and fun — but too much can spike blood sugar and cause health problems, especially in **dwarf hamsters** who are prone to diabetes.

Safe Fruits (Very Small Amounts):

- Apple (no seeds)

- Banana

- Blueberry

- Raspberry

- Strawberry

- Pear (no seeds)

One berry or a single thin slice of apple is plenty — **once or twice a week** max.

Protein Treats: Not Just for Bodybuilders

Wild hamsters eat insects, grubs, and other small protein sources. Your pet hamster needs **a bit of extra protein**, especially when growing, recovering from illness, or nursing.

Safe Protein Sources:

- **Mealworms** (dried or live)
- **Boiled egg** (no salt or seasoning)
- **Cooked chicken** (plain, tiny amounts)
- **Plain tofu**
- **Dry dog kibble** (check ingredients first)

Offer protein treats **1–2 times per week** in small amounts.

Treats: What's Okay (And What's Just Sugar in Disguise)

You can find "hamster treats" in stores, but read the labels carefully — many are loaded with honey, molasses, yogurt, or colored bits that do nothing but spike blood sugar.

Acceptable Treats (Occasionally):

- Unsweetened whole-grain cereal (like a Cheerio)
- Sunflower seeds (a few only — high in fat)
- Pumpkin seeds
- Plain popcorn (air-popped, no salt or butter)
- Unsalted plain nuts (tiny amounts only)

Treats to Avoid:

- Yogurt drops

- Store-bought honey sticks

- Sugary fruit mixes

- Human junk food

- Anything sticky or chewy

If your hamster starts ignoring its regular food in favor of treats — **dial it back.**

What NOT to Feed (Ever)

Some foods are outright dangerous.

Never Feed:

- Chocolate

- Garlic

- Onion

- Citrus fruits

- Almonds

- Raw beans or potatoes

- Rhubarb

- Anything spicy, salty, or seasoned

And absolutely **no alcohol, caffeine, dairy desserts, or fried food.**

Feeding Tips & Daily Routine

- Feed once daily, ideally in the evening when your hamster is waking up

- Remove uneaten fresh food after 3–4 hours

- Keep dry food in a **clean bowl** or **scatter-feed** to encourage natural foraging

- Wash water bottles/dishes regularly and refill daily

- Observe eating habits — sudden changes may mean illness

Summary: What Helps, What Harms

Helps	Harms
Balanced seed mix or pellets	Sugary yogurt drops
Fresh veg (small amounts)	Chocolate, citrus, garlic
Occasional fruit or protein	Too much fruit or fatty treats
Clean water daily	Dirty dishes or old produce
Food rotation and foraging	Feeding only one type of food

Your hamster's health starts with what you put in the food bowl. A little knowledge goes a long way — and now you've got it.

Next, we'll explore your daily hamster routine: handling, bonding, and what to expect from day-to-day life.

5

Daily Life with a Hamster – Routine, Handling & Bonding

Hamsters don't come with a user manual — but if they did, this would be it.

You've got the cage. You've got the food. You're probably staring at your new roommate, wondering, "Now what?" This chapter covers exactly what to do once your hamster is home: from handling and bonding to setting a routine that keeps both of you happy.

Because as cute as they are, hamsters aren't toys. They're living creatures with quirks, moods, and personal space issues. Treat them right, and you'll have a tiny, fuzzy friend who actually wants to interact with you.

Your First Week: Don't Rush It

The first week is not about playing — it's about letting your hamster **settle in**.

What to do (and not do) during week one:

- Give them peace and quiet

- Avoid loud noises or sudden movements

- Refill food and water without trying to touch them

- Spot-clean only — no full cage cleaning yet

- Don't try to pick them up

- Don't poke around their hideout

- Don't let kids or pets near the cage constantly

They're in a brand-new world. Everything smells strange. Everything sounds huge. Let them adjust, and they'll trust you faster.

Establishing a Routine

Hamsters thrive on consistency. They're creatures of habit — and your job is to build habits that keep them safe, clean, and stress-free.

Daily:

- Check food and water

- Remove soiled bedding

- Give fresh veg (small amount)

- Quietly talk to your hamster while they're awake

- Offer your hand (flat) near the cage for scent familiarity

Weekly:

- Spot clean cage

- Refresh sand bath

- Rotate toys or enrichment items

Monthly:

- Full cage clean (swap bedding, clean surfaces)

- Deep clean toys, wheel, and accessories

Keep your schedule consistent. Over time, your hamster will begin to recognize your voice, scent, and rhythm — that's where bonding starts.

Bonding: From Stranger to Friend

Hamsters don't bond like dogs. You won't get tail wags and kisses. But they do recognize their humans, and with time, they'll come to trust you — even enjoy your presence.

Step-by-Step Bonding:

1. **Hand in Cage Method:** Rest your clean, dry hand flat inside the cage daily. Let your hamster sniff, climb, or ignore it. Don't chase or poke.

2. **Treat Luring:** Offer treats from your fingertips. Let them approach on their terms.

3. **Scoop, Don't Grab:** When they're comfortable, gently scoop them up with both hands like a bowl. Never grab from above — that triggers predator fear.

4. **Short Handling Sessions:** Begin with just 30 seconds. Build slowly. Let them walk across your lap or arms.

5. **Talk to Them:** Your voice becomes familiar and calming — use it often, especially before handling.

It may take days, weeks, or even longer depending on the hamster's temperament. Don't rush. Trust is earned.

Handling Do's and Don'ts

Do	Don't
Scoop gently with both hands	Grab from above like a claw
Handle low to the ground	Hold over hard floors or tables
Handle when hamster is awake	Wake them up to play
Let them walk across your hands	Trap them or squeeze tightly
Watch their body language	Ignore signs of stress or fear

Some hamsters are bold and curious. Others are shy and skittish. Work with the personality you've got, not the one you hoped for.

Signs Your Hamster Trusts You

- Takes treats from your hand

- Climbs into your palm voluntarily

- Grooms or stretches while you're nearby

- Doesn't flinch when you approach

- Sleeps out in the open (big sign of trust)

If your hamster does any of these, congrats — you're officially part of the club.

When Things Go Wrong: Biting, Hiding, Screaming

Yep, hamsters scream. It sounds like a squeaky horror movie — and it means they're terrified.

Common mistakes:

- Picking them up too soon

- Chasing them around the cage

- Ignoring their body language

- Handling during the day (they're groggy and grumpy)

If Your Hamster Bites:

- **Don't punish or yell.**

- **Don't jerk your hand away suddenly.**

- **Wash and disinfect the bite.**

- Rewind the bonding process — they need more time.

Even the tamest hamster can nip if they're startled. Be calm, predictable, and patient.

Interaction Time: What Counts as Quality Time?

You don't need to spend hours a day entertaining your hamster. **15–30 minutes of gentle interaction** in the evening is plenty.

- Sit beside the cage and talk

- Offer a treat or let them sniff your hands

- Set up a safe playpen or bathtub play area

- Let them explore your hands and lap (supervised!)

Never leave a hamster unattended during out-of-cage time. They're fast, sneaky, and full of escape artist energy.

Summary: Life with a Hamster, Day by Day

- Give your hamster **time to adjust** — don't rush bonding

- Keep a **consistent daily routine** — feeding, cleaning, calm presence

- Learn **safe handling techniques** — no grabbing, no startling

- Let trust build slowly — some hamsters take time

- Observe behavior — it's how they communicate

- Respect their **natural rhythm** — they're crepuscular, not toys

You're not just taking care of a pet — you're building a quiet, respectful relationship with a tiny roommate. Handle that well, and you'll be amazed at how much personality lives inside that little ball of fluff.

6

Hamster Health & Hygiene – Spotting Illness, Vet Visits & First Aid

Hamsters are pretty tough for their size, but they're not invincible. When they get sick, they often hide it — a survival instinct left over from the wild (where showing weakness can make you dinner).

So, as a hamster owner, your job is to become part detective, part nurse, and part spa manager. This chapter will help you recognize early signs of illness, keep your hamster clean and healthy, and know when it's time to call a vet.

Know What "Normal" Looks Like First

You can't spot a problem if you don't know what normal looks like. Get familiar with your hamster's:

- **Activity level** (most active at dusk and dawn)

- **Appetite and drinking habits**

- **Poop and pee output** (yes, you should look)

- **Fur texture and grooming**

- **Eyes, ears, and nose (clear, no crust)**

Check on your hamster daily — even if it's just a quick visual scan while they stretch, eat, or run on the wheel.

Common Signs of Illness

If your hamster shows any of the following signs, something might be wrong:

Possible Illness Sign	What It Might Mean
Lethargy (sudden)	Infection, pain, dehydration
Not eating or drinking	Dental problems, illness
Hunched posture	Abdominal pain, distress
Wet tail or diarrhea	Potentially fatal condition (see below)
Labored breathing	Respiratory infection
Clicking or wheezing	Lung issue or respiratory irritation
Bald patches or scabs	Mites, ringworm, overgrooming
Overgrown teeth	Dental imbalance (can't eat)
Red, crusty eyes	Conjunctivitis, allergy
Excessive itching	Parasites or dry skin
Swelling or lumps	Tumors, abscesses, cysts

If you're unsure — **assume it's serious.** Hamsters can go downhill fast.

Wet Tail: The One You Need to Know About

"Wet tail" isn't just a gross-sounding phrase — it's a dangerous condition, especially in young hamsters.

What is it?

- A **bacterial infection** of the intestines
- Causes **diarrhea, dehydration, weakness, and a wet, dirty rear**

Symptoms:

- Wetness or staining near tail
- Strong, foul smell
- Lethargy, loss of appetite
- Hunched posture

What to Do:

- **Immediate vet visit.**
- Isolate the hamster (if housed with others)
- Keep them warm, hydrated, and stress-free

Without treatment, wet tail can be fatal within 48 hours.

When to See a Vet (And Why You Should)

Hamsters may be small, but they still deserve real medical care. If you notice **persistent or worsening symptoms**, it's time to find a vet.

Reasons to visit a vet:

- Diarrhea or dehydration

- Cuts, swelling, or bleeding

- Respiratory issues

- Sudden weight loss

- Trouble eating

- Unusual behavior or posture

Find a "Small Animal" or "Exotics" Vet

Not all vets treat hamsters. Call ahead and ask:

"Do you treat small mammals or exotic rodents like hamsters?"

Keep the number handy in case of emergencies.

First Aid: What You Can Do at Home (And What You Shouldn't)

There's only so much home care you can safely provide. Still, it helps to have a **small pet first aid kit** for minor issues.

Good to Have On Hand:

- Clean gauze pads

- Cotton swabs

- Small nail clippers

- Pet-safe antiseptic (no alcohol or hydrogen peroxide)

- Syringe/dropper (for water/meds)

- Digital scale (to monitor weight)

What You Should NOT Do:

- Don't give human medications
- Don't apply creams without vet approval
- Don't delay vet visits hoping it "goes away"
- Don't use essential oils or home remedies (many are toxic)

Grooming Basics (Yes, Even Hamsters Need TLC)

Most hamsters groom themselves — obsessively. But occasionally, you may need to help out.

Nail Trimming:

- Only if they're **overgrown or curling**
- Use **small animal nail clippers**
- Only trim the **clear tip** — avoid the pink quick
- If nervous, ask a vet or groomer to show you first

Fur Brushing (Long-haired Syrians only):

- Use a soft toothbrush or tiny pet comb
- Brush gently to prevent tangles
- Never bathe in water — it removes natural oils and causes stress

Sand Baths (as covered earlier):

- Keeps their fur clean
- Reduces oil buildup and itching
- Let them roll in it — don't dump it on them

Cage Cleaning & Hygiene

Cleanliness prevents illness — but overcleaning causes stress. Balance is key.

Spot Clean Daily:

- Remove soiled bedding
- Clean around water and food areas
- Scoop out old veggies

Full Clean Every 4–6 Weeks:

- Remove 80–90% of bedding (leave a little to preserve scent)
- Wash cage with mild soap or pet-safe cleaner
- Rinse thoroughly
- Replace dry, fresh bedding
- Put everything back where it was — hamsters like consistency

Don't deep-clean weekly unless absolutely needed. Overcleaning can make your hamster feel like its home is constantly being destroyed.

Summary: Staying Healthy, the Hamster Way

Do This	Avoid This
Watch daily for behavior changes	Ignoring small symptoms
Keep cage clean and well-ventilated	Overcleaning too often
Provide sand baths and chew toys	Bathing in water or scented bedding
Visit an exotics vet when needed	Giving human medicine or guessing
Keep a first aid kit ready	Waiting too long to act

Hamsters can't tell you when something's wrong — but they'll show you if you know what to look for. Early action saves lives (and vet bills).

7

Hamster Hygiene – Cleaning, Grooming & Cage Freshness

Your hamster won't be lining up for a bubble bath anytime soon. But that doesn't mean hygiene doesn't matter.

A clean, well-kept hamster is a healthy hamster — and thankfully, their self-grooming instincts do most of the heavy lifting. Still, as the responsible human in the relationship, **you've got a few important jobs**: keeping the cage fresh, trimming when needed, and avoiding common hygiene mistakes.

This chapter is all about how to keep your hamster (and their habitat) fresh, safe, and stink-free — without stressing them out or over-cleaning.

Let's Get This Straight: Hamsters Don't Smell (If You're Doing It Right)

A healthy hamster in a properly set-up cage with the right bedding and routine cleaning will not stink.

What *does* smell:

- Dirty bedding soaked with urine

- Rotten veggies left in the cage

- Small cages that don't allow for proper burrowing

- Poor ventilation

So if your hamster smells like a public restroom — the problem isn't the hamster. It's probably the housing.

Daily Spot Cleaning

This is the hamster version of tidying up the house.

Do This Daily:

- Remove soiled bedding (check corners they pee in)

- Throw out any uneaten fresh food

- Check and clean the sand bath if it's used as a litter box

- Wipe up any obvious messes around the water bottle

Use tissue or a small scoop — keep it fast, gentle, and non-invasive. This keeps things clean **without disrupting their entire environment**.

Full Cage Cleaning: How Often & How Thorough?

A deep clean should not happen weekly unless absolutely needed. Why?

Because **hamsters rely on scent** to feel safe. If you wipe away everything they know, it's like replacing their house every Sunday — no fun.

Deep Clean Schedule:

- **Every 4–6 weeks** is usually enough

- Clean earlier if there's illness, parasites, or unusual smell

How to Clean:

1. Remove your hamster to a safe playpen or travel cage

2. Scoop out 80–90% of the bedding

3. Leave a handful of old bedding to preserve scent

4. Wash the cage with warm water and mild soap (or pet-safe cleaner)

5. Rinse and dry thoroughly

6. Wash wheel, hideouts, dishes, and sand bath

7. Reassemble cage with clean bedding — try to keep layout familiar

8. Return your hamster with minimal fanfare

Don't forget to clean **under the wheel** — it's often a secret pee spot.

Scent Marking vs. "Dirty" – Know the Difference

Sometimes new hamster owners think their hamster has a skin problem or is dirty — but it's often just **scent gland residue.**

Syrian hamsters:

- Have scent glands on each hip

- May leave little yellowish patches on bedding or decor

- Males often mark more than females

Dwarf hamsters have a scent gland on their belly. You may see them rubbing it on things — this is normal behavior, not a mess.

Sand Baths: Hamster Hygiene Essential

As covered before, hamsters don't need water baths. **They bathe in sand — like tiny desert spa-goers.**

Setup:

- Container large enough for full-body rolling

- 1–2 inches of fine, dust-free sand

- Leave it in the cage 24/7 or offer a few times a week

Approved Sand:

- Chinchilla **sand** (not dust!)

- Reptile sand with no calcium additives

- Sterilized children's play sand (baked at 200°C/400°F for 30 minutes)

Clean regularly:

- Sift out poop and clumps

- Fully replace once a week

Your hamster will use it for grooming, digging, and sometimes even as a litter box.

Grooming Long-Haired Hamsters

Most hamsters don't need brushing — **except long-haired Syrians.**

What You'll Need:

- A soft toothbrush or baby comb

- Patience (and maybe a snack bribe)

How to Groom:

- Brush gently, especially around the rear

- Trim any matted fur if necessary (carefully!)

- Avoid getting fur wet — it mats easily

- Keep bedding type in mind (paper-based is less likely to tangle than hay or wood)

Long-haired males may drag bedding or poop in their coats — keep an eye out.

Nail Trimming: Rare, But Sometimes Needed

Most hamsters wear their nails down naturally. But sometimes, especially with less climbing or digging enrichment, **nails can overgrow.**

Signs nails are too long:

- Curling or catching on fabric

- Hamster limping or nibbling feet

- Scratching themselves excessively

How to Trim (If Needed):

1. Wrap hamster gently in a soft towel burrito

2. Use small animal or baby nail clippers

3. Clip **just the tip** — avoid the pink quick

4. Ask a vet or experienced groomer for help if unsure

Never use human-sized nail clippers or scissors. If you're shaky or nervous, skip it and get professional help.

Things to Never Do (Seriously, Don't)

- Don't give your hamster a water bath — it can lead to hypothermia, stress, or shock

- Don't use essential oils or scented bedding — hamsters have ultra-sensitive noses

- Don't use strong cleaners like bleach or vinegar

- Don't over-clean — it's stressful and disorienting

- Don't forget to wash your hands before and after handling

Summary: Clean, But Not Sterile

Do This	Avoid This
Spot clean daily	Full clean every few days
Use safe bedding and rotate sand	Fluffy cotton or scented bedding
Deep clean every 4–6 weeks	Removing all bedding at once
Brush long-haired hamsters weekly	Cutting fur without checking
Monitor nails and trim carefully	Ignoring overgrown claws
Let your hamster do most of the grooming	Bathing in water or soap

A clean hamster is a healthy hamster. But more importantly, **a clean environment** keeps their stress low and their immune system strong.

Keep it simple, consistent, and scent-friendly — your hamster will thank you (in its own quiet way).

8

Enrichment & Toys – How to Keep Your Hamster Happy (and Busy)

A bored hamster is a destructive hamster. Chewing the bars? Climbing the water bottle? Sleeping all day? That's not just "hamster stuff." It's usually a **screaming sign** that your pet is under-stimulated.

Hamsters may be small, but they're smart, curious, and wired for adventure — especially at night. They need a dynamic, interesting environment to keep their body active and brain engaged. In this chapter, we'll cover how to enrich your hamster's life without filling the cage with overpriced plastic.

What Is Enrichment, Really?

Enrichment just means **giving your hamster opportunities to do hamster things**:

- Dig

- Chew

- Climb

- Explore

- Forage

- Nest

These are **instinctual behaviors**, not "bonus" features. Without outlets for them, your hamster may develop stress behaviors or health issues.

Types of Enrichment (And How to Do It Right)

1. Chewing

Hamster teeth never stop growing. If they don't chew regularly, they can develop painful dental problems.

Great chew options:

- Apple wood sticks

- Whimzee dog chews (small sizes only — safe and fun to shred)

- Cardboard (toilet paper rolls, egg cartons)

- Coconut shells

- Hardwood blocks (untreated, unpainted)

Avoid painted wood, pine cones, or soft plastic toys — many are toxic or splinter.

2. Burrowing

In the wild, hamsters build **elaborate underground tunnels**. If you only provide a thin layer of bedding, you're denying one of their most natural joys.

How to support burrowing:

- Minimum **6 inches of bedding** — 10–12 is better

- Use paper-based bedding or a mix of paper and aspen for structure

- Create a "dig zone" by piling bedding in one area

- Bury treats and toys for added fun

Pro tip: Add tunnels or tubes **under** the bedding to encourage deeper burrows.

3. Foraging

Hamsters don't naturally eat from a bowl. In the wild, they spend hours sniffing, digging, and stashing food.

How to encourage foraging:

- Scatter food across the bedding instead of using a bowl

- Use small cardboard boxes or DIY puzzles with food inside

- Hide sunflower seeds in toilet rolls or hay piles

- Rotate hiding spots weekly to keep things interesting

This stimulates both their body and brain — and they love the challenge.

4. Climbing

Some hamsters (especially dwarfs) love to climb. Others (like Syrians) are a bit less graceful. But a little vertical variety can go a long way.

Safe climbing structures:

- Cork logs

- Wooden bridges

- Platforms with ramps (not too high)

- Branches (cleaned and untreated)

Avoid tall cages and vertical drops — hamsters have **terrible depth perception**, and a fall from even 12 inches can cause serious injury.

5. Exploration

Your hamster's cage is home base — but supervised out-of-cage time can be a great way to add adventure.

Options:

- A safe playpen or dry bathtub with toys and tunnels

- A DIY maze made from cardboard

- Dig boxes filled with paper shreds, sand, or foraging material

Never leave your hamster unattended outside the cage. **No couches, no floors, no escape routes.**

And no, exercise balls are *not* a safe alternative — more on that below.

The Great Exercise Ball Debate (Spoiler: Just Say No)

Exercise balls are often marketed as "fun" and "safe." In reality, they're…

- Poorly ventilated

- Disorienting

- Hard to steer

- Easily crashed into walls or furniture

- Known to cause stress, injuries, and broken toenails

Hamsters **can't see well**, and spinning inside a plastic orb with no escape is not exercise — it's hamster bumper cars in a panic room.

Stick with a proper wheel, safe playpens, and enrichment. Skip the ball.

How to Rotate Toys (Without Going Broke)

You don't need a toy aisle explosion. You just need **variety**.

Rotation ideas:

- Swap out 2–3 toys every week

- Rearrange tunnels or platforms

- Introduce simple DIY puzzles (cardboard boxes with holes and hidden food)

- Change hideout locations to mimic "moving burrows"

This keeps things fresh without needing to buy new gear constantly. Your hamster won't get bored — and neither will you.

Enrichment Checklist

Let's summarize what a hamster-friendly cage should offer:

Behavior	Enrichment Tool
Chewing	Apple wood, Whimzees, cardboard
Burrowing	Deep bedding, dig boxes
Foraging	Scatter feeding, hidden treats
Climbing	Logs, ramps, low platforms
Nesting	Nesting paper, soft hay, hideouts
Exploring	Playpen time, tunnels, mazes

Aim for at least **3 types of enrichment in the cage at all times.**

Summary: A Happy Hamster Is a Busy Hamster

- Hamsters need stimulation — mentally *and* physically

- Offer variety: chew toys, tunnels, dig spots, and puzzle feeders

- Don't overcrowd the cage — leave room to move

- Rotate enrichment weekly to prevent boredom

- Avoid unsafe items like plastic wheels, tall platforms, and exercise balls

- Watch your hamster — they'll show you what they love

Enrichment isn't a luxury. It's how you turn a cage into a home — one that's full of adventure, comfort, and joy.

9

Taming & Trust – How to Build a Bond That Lasts

Some people get lucky. They bring home a fearless hamster who practically somersaults into their hand.

Most of us... don't.

Taming a hamster takes time, patience, and a bit of psychology. They're prey animals — hardwired to run from anything bigger than a shoebox (like you). This chapter walks you through exactly how to **earn your hamster's trust**, read its body language, and become more than just "the giant who brings food."

Step 1: Understand Their Mindset

Hamsters don't bite out of meanness — they bite out of fear. They're not ignoring you because they hate you — they're watching you from the shadows, calculating whether you're safe.

The key to taming is **respecting their natural instincts** while gradually proving you're not a threat.

Step 2: Let Them Settle First (Seriously, Don't Skip This)

The biggest mistake new owners make?

Trying to handle the hamster the day they bring it home.

Give your hamster at least **3–5 days to settle in** without handling. This helps reduce stress and lets them get used to:

- New smells

- New sounds

- The layout of their home

- Your presence nearby

During this time, quietly talk to them, sit by the cage, and let them hear your voice. Let them come to you.

Step 3: The Hand-Taming Process (Day-by-Day Guide)

This is the slow-cooked bonding method — not microwave love.

Day 1–3: Presence

- Sit by the cage while they're awake (usually evening)

- Talk softly — read aloud, narrate what you're doing

- Let them get used to your scent and voice

- Don't reach in yet

Day 4–7: Scent and Curiosity

- Wash your hands with unscented soap

- Place your clean hand flat inside the cage, palm up

- Let your hamster sniff, ignore, or crawl on it (no grabbing!)

- Offer a treat from your palm — millet, sunflower seed, etc.

- Do this daily for 5–10 minutes

Week 2: Gentle Scooping

- When your hamster regularly approaches your hand, try scooping them **with two hands, like a bowl**

- Keep it low — over bedding or your lap

- Handle for short sessions (1–2 minutes)

- Always reward with a treat afterward

Week 3 and Beyond: Exploration Time

- Let them walk over your hands, lap, or in a playpen

- Be consistent — short, positive sessions daily

- Gradually extend the length of handling

Never chase or trap them. Always let them approach **on their terms**.

Tips for Successful Taming

Be consistent – Daily short sessions work better than long weekly ones

Use positive reinforcement – Reward calm behavior with small treats

Handle at the right time – Early evening is best when they're naturally active

Start in the cage – Let them get used to your hand before you lift them

Use a safe space – A playpen or dry bathtub is great for taming sessions

Stay calm – If you're nervous, they'll sense it

And above all: **don't rush it**. Every hamster is different. Some bond in days. Others take weeks — or longer.

What If They Bite?

It happens. It doesn't mean you've failed. Most bites are because of:

- **Fear** – You moved too fast

- **Scent confusion** – Hands smelled like food

- **Surprise** – Woke them up too suddenly

What to Do:

- Stay calm — don't jerk your hand or shout

- Gently set them down

- Wash and disinfect the bite

- Rewind the bonding process a step or two

Never punish a hamster for biting. It'll only make them fear you more.

What Trust Looks Like

When your hamster trusts you, you'll notice:

- They take food from your hand without hesitation

- They climb onto you voluntarily

- They let you scoop them without panic

- They groom themselves in front of you (a sign of feeling safe)

- They sleep in more exposed spots (a big trust signal)

Congratulations — you've earned their trust. Now the real fun begins.

Summary: From Stranger to Friend

- Let your hamster **settle in** before attempting to handle

- Use your **voice, scent, and treats** to build familiarity

- Never rush taming — go at their pace, not yours

- Be patient, consistent, and gentle

- Learn to **read their body language** and respond appropriately

- Celebrate the small wins — every step builds the bond

Taming isn't just about getting your hamster to tolerate you — it's about building a relationship based on trust and respect. And once you have that, the reward is a confident, curious little companion who's happy to share their tiny world with you.

10

Handling & Playtime – Safe, Fun, and Stress-Free Interaction

You've earned your hamster's trust. They know your scent. They don't flinch when you approach. You've reached the "friends with paws" stage.

Now it's time to make interaction fun — not just for them, but for you too.

This final chapter covers **how to handle your hamster safely,** create engaging playtime routines, and build a real-life connection that doesn't involve tiptoeing around a cage with a sunflower seed every night.

Handling Basics: Do It Right, or Don't Do It at All

A calm, well-handled hamster is a confident hamster. A startled, dropped, or grabbed hamster becomes nervous — sometimes for life.

How to Handle Safely:

- Wash hands first (unscented soap only)

- Scoop gently with **both hands cupped like a bowl**

- Keep hands **low over bedding** when lifting — no mid-air juggling

- Let the hamster **climb into your hands voluntarily** when possible

- Always move **slowly and predictably**

If they seem unsure, back off and try again later. No need to force it.

How Long Can You Handle a Hamster?

Start small: **1–2 minutes**, then increase gradually as your hamster gets more comfortable.

Signs to Stop:

- Biting or struggling

- Sudden freezing

- Excessive jumping or trying to escape

- Teeth chattering

- Stressed breathing or squirming

If they start showing stress signals, give them a break and return them to the cage calmly.

Playtime Outside the Cage: Setup for Success

You don't need to unleash your hamster on the living room carpet (and you really shouldn't). A secure, contained play space gives them a change of scenery **without risking your sanity**.

Great Play Areas:

- A dry, empty bathtub (plug the drain!)

- A secure hamster playpen

- A large plastic storage bin (with high sides)

- A DIY cardboard maze or "hamster gym"

Never allow free-roaming on open floors, couches, or beds — hamsters are fast, fearless, and fond of vanishing into walls.

Playtime Ideas (They're Smarter Than You Think)

Hamsters love:

- Cardboard tunnels and boxes

- Toilet roll mazes

- Scatter feeding for foraging

- Digging zones with shredded paper

- Climbing platforms

- Hiding snacks under small flower pots

Rotate toys weekly to keep things fresh. They'll engage more when things feel new.

How Often Should You Handle or Play?

Aim for **15–30 minutes of gentle interaction per evening**. That can include:

- Handling

- Talking softly

- Letting them explore a playpen

- Offering food by hand

You don't need to play for hours — just **consistent, low-stress bonding time** makes a big difference.

Supervision is Non-Negotiable

Hamsters are:

- Small

- Silent

- Sneaky

- Sudden runners

Always supervise out-of-cage play. Even in a playpen, keep an eye out for climbing attempts or potential escape routes. And **never leave them alone near other pets or children** — even "gentle" animals can accidentally harm them.

When They Don't Want to Play

Sometimes your hamster just isn't in the mood. That's okay.

Respect their body language:

- If they hide when you approach

- If they seem groggy or irritable

- If they freeze or bite

Let them be. Try again later. Just like people, they have off days.

Final Safety Tips

Do	Don't
Handle over soft surfaces	Hold over hard floors or tables
Use two hands to scoop	Grab from above like a claw
Keep sessions short at first	Force handling if they resist
Set up a secure playpen	Let them roam the floor or furniture
Be consistent	Handle only once in a blue moon

Summary: Handling Done Right

- Build trust **before** handling

- Use **gentle, cupped hands**, not a grabbing motion

- Keep handling **short, calm, and consistent**

- Create safe, enriching **out-of-cage play spaces**

- Supervise every second — no exceptions

- Let your hamster **lead the pace** of interaction

A well-handled hamster is more than just a cute pet — they're a relaxed, curious little companion who actually looks forward to seeing you.

And that's the real reward: not just owning a hamster... but being part of their tiny, wonderful world.

11

Understanding Hamster Behavior – What They're Really Saying

Hamsters can't talk. But they do communicate — loudly, if you know how to listen.

From squeaks to stares, bar chewing to backflips, your hamster is constantly trying to tell you how it feels. The problem is, most humans have no idea what any of it means. This chapter teaches you how to **read your hamster's body language and behavior**, so you can respond like a trusted companion — not a clueless roommate.

Why This Matters

Hamsters are prey animals. They don't usually scream when they're in trouble or stressed — they **show it** through behavior.

Understanding these signs helps you:

- Build trust faster

- Spot early signs of illness or discomfort

- Avoid accidentally stressing them out

- Improve your bond and daily interaction

The Basics of Hamster Body Language

Let's start with the common postures and what they really mean:

Body Language	What It Likely Means
Ears forward, sniffing	Curious, interested
Ears back, crouching	Nervous or unsure
Standing up on hind legs	Alert, investigating sounds or smells
Freezing suddenly	Sensed danger — evaluating the situation
Teeth chattering	Warning sign — back off!
Lying flat, belly down	Submitting, scared, or overheated
Grooming in front of you	Feeling calm and safe
Running and hiding	Overstimulated or scared
Staring at you silently	Processing — could mean curiosity or wariness

A calm hamster will act slowly, sniff a lot, and explore. A stressed one will either freeze, bolt, or repeat weird patterns (more on that below).

Vocalizations: The Rare But Telling Sounds

Hamsters aren't very chatty — but when they *do* make noise, it usually means something.

Sound	Meaning
Squeaking	Mild protest, excitement, or play — often during taming or handling
Screaming	Full panic or pain — extremely rare and serious
Teeth clicking/chattering	Back off immediately — your hamster is annoyed or scared
Chirping (soft, high-pitched)	Dwarf hamsters may chirp during social grooming or play

If your hamster screams, it's terrified — not mad. It's not a tantrum; it's a trauma response. Stop what you're doing and give it space.

Weird Behaviors (That Actually Make Sense)

Hamsters have quirks. Some look odd, some look alarming. Here's what's normal, what's not, and how to tell:

Bar Chewing

- **Why it happens**: Boredom, frustration, small cage
- **What to do**: Upgrade cage size, add enrichment, give chew toys

- **Note**: If it continues, consider switching to a tank-style cage

Cage Zoomies

- **Why it happens**: Excess energy or stress (often after a cage clean)

- **What to do**: Let it pass — it's usually temporary. Provide more digging, foraging, or playtime.

Monkey Barr-ing (Climbing the bars repeatedly)

- **Why it happens**: Boredom or cage is too small

- **What to do**: Add climbing toys, check cage size, rotate enrichment

Sleeping in Odd Places

- **Why it happens**: Too hot, too bright, new environment

- **What to do**: Make sure the nest area is dark, safe, and cool

Hoarding Everything

- **Why it happens**: Totally normal — they hoard food, bedding, even toys

- **What to do**: Let them. Don't clear out the stash unless it's molding.

Burying Their Food Bowl

- **Why it happens**: They're nesting around the scent or protecting their stash

- **What to do**: Scatter feed or let them keep playing home decorator

Signs of Fear vs. Trust

It's easy to misread a scared hamster as "not in the mood." Here's a quick guide to what fear looks like — and what trust looks like.

Trust	Fear
Approaches you	Runs away immediately
Climbs onto hand	Hides in corner
Grooms while you watch	Freezes stiffly when you enter
Sleeps in the open	Sleeps buried deep or in awkward spots
Explores cage confidently	Stays in one spot for long periods

If you notice fearful behaviors frequently, **review your handling process**, cage setup, or possible stressors like noise, pets, or drafts.

What About Dwarf Hamsters?

Dwarf hamsters, especially robos and Chinese dwarfs, are often more skittish and fast-moving. Their body language tends to be subtler, but the principles are the same:

- **Trust takes longer**

- **Movements are faster and more sudden**

- **They often chirp or squeak more than Syrians**

Don't mistake speed for confidence — some dwarfs will zoom away the second they're touched, even if they like you.

Behavior & Environment: Everything's Connected

A lot of behavioral issues aren't "personality problems." They're **housing or enrichment problems**.

Check your basics:

- Is the cage at least 450 square inches?

- Is there deep bedding for digging?

- Is the wheel big and solid (not wire)?

- Is there variety in toys, chews, and tunnels?

- Is the room quiet, dim, and free of loud vibrations?

Fix the environment first — you'd be surprised how many "problem behaviors" vanish when your hamster's home finally meets their needs.

Summary: Listen With Your Eyes

Hamsters may be tiny, but they're expressive. You just need to know what to watch for:

- Pay attention to posture, movement, and activity

- Vocal sounds are rare, but important

- Weird habits often reflect boredom or stress

- Fear and trust look different — learn the signs

- Fix the **environment** first if behavior seems off

Understanding your hamster's behavior is the difference between just keeping a pet… and actually connecting with one.

12

Hamsters & Kids – How to Keep It Safe, Fun & Respectful

Hamsters are often bought *for* kids — but here's the catch: hamsters aren't children's pets. They're tiny, nocturnal prey animals with **fast reflexes, delicate bodies, and serious boundaries**.

Does that mean kids and hamsters don't mix? Not at all. It just means the adults need to lead the way — by setting realistic expectations, teaching gentle handling, and supervising every interaction.

This chapter is your full guide to creating a safe, happy relationship between your hamster and the younger humans in the house.

First Things First: A Reality Check

Let's be blunt.

Hamsters are:

- **Nocturnal** (awake when kids are asleep)

- **Skittish** (don't like loud noises or sudden movement)

- **Fast and fragile** (easy to drop, hurt, or scare)

- **Easily stressed** (and stress = illness in hamsters)

They are not:

- Cuddly, tolerant lap pets

- "Starter pets" for toddlers

- Okay being poked, squeezed, or woken up mid-day

- Able to defend themselves if mishandled

If a child wants a pet to snuggle, follow them around, or play fetch — this isn't it.

But if you're ready to **teach respect, empathy, and care**, a hamster can become a magical learning companion.

What Age Is Appropriate?

Generally, **age 8 and up** is the earliest a child can begin learning proper hamster care — **with adult supervision.**

Younger kids can still enjoy the experience, but they should **never be the primary caregiver**. The adult must remain in charge of:

- Feeding

- Cleaning

- Health checks

- Handling (unless the child has proven gentleness over time)

Think of it as **a family pet** that the child can enjoy — not one they're responsible for alone.

Setting the Right Expectations

Before you even bring the hamster home, sit down with your child and explain:

- Hamsters are **awake at night**

- Hamsters don't like being woken up

- Hamsters are fast and fragile

- We need to **earn their trust** over time

- We must always use **gentle voices and slow hands**

You'd be amazed how well most kids respond to this when they're treated like smart little humans instead of just excited customers.

How to Involve Kids (Safely & Respectfully)

Even younger children can:

- Help choose toys and bedding

- Watch during playpen time

- Help refill food and water (with supervision)

- Gently offer treats

- Watch taming sessions

- Help decorate or rearrange the cage (outside the cage)

Let them observe first. Then guide them through supervised interaction. Praise calm, slow behavior — and gently correct anything rough.

Handling Rules for Kids

Here's the non-negotiable list:

1. Always sit down low (on the floor or couch with a towel)
2. Only handle when the hamster is **awake and alert**
3. Always use **two hands like a scoop** — never grab
4. No chasing the hamster around the cage
5. No poking, tapping, or yelling
6. Put the hamster down immediately if it squirms or tries to escape

7. Wash hands before and after

If they can't follow these rules consistently, they're **not ready to handle yet** — and that's okay. Watching is still learning.

Teaching Empathy Through Hamster Care

This is where hamsters truly shine for kids.

Because they're small, quiet, and easily frightened, kids have to learn:

- Patience

- Respect for boundaries

- Listening with their eyes

- Understanding non-verbal cues

- That trust is earned, not given

Hamsters give **immediate feedback**. Treat them well, and they'll come closer. Rush or scare them, and they'll hide. It's a powerful lesson in cause and effect.

When Things Go Wrong

Let's be real — accidents happen. If a child drops the hamster, forgets to close the cage lid, or pokes too hard:

- Stay calm

- Check the hamster for injury

- Use it as a gentle teaching moment

- Don't punish — guide

Hamsters are forgiving creatures — and so are kids, when they're given the chance to learn responsibly.

Summary: Hamsters + Kids Can Work (With Adults in Charge)

Good Ideas	Not-So-Good Ideas
Supervised handling	Letting kids carry them around alone
Teaching trust and respect	Treating the hamster like a toy
Letting kids help with feeding and enrichment	Making kids fully responsible
Watching playtime together	Leaving cage near loud, chaotic areas
Talking about body language and feelings	Expecting cuddles and tricks

With the right guidance, a hamster can help a child develop empathy, patience, and genuine interest in animal care — lessons that last far beyond the cage.

13

Saying Goodbye – Lifespan, Death & Grieving

No one likes to think about it, but the truth is: **hamsters don't live long**.

Most live only **2 to 3 years**, sometimes a bit longer with good care and a bit of luck. Their lives are brief, but they leave a surprisingly big hole in the hearts of the people who love them.

This chapter helps you understand what to expect as your hamster ages, how to handle the end of life with compassion, and how to support kids (and yourself) through the grief that follows.

How Long Do Hamsters Live?

- **Syrian hamsters**: 2–3 years (occasionally 3.5)

- **Dwarf hamsters**: 1.5–2.5 years

- **Roborovski dwarfs**: Can reach 3+ years, but it's rare

- **Chinese hamsters**: Often 2–3 years

Hamsters age quickly. A 2-year-old hamster is roughly equivalent to a human in their late 80s. As they reach the end of their life, you'll start to see signs — subtle at first, then more obvious.

Signs of Aging

You may notice:

- Slower movements

- Less interest in play

- Thinning fur

- Weight loss

- Sleeping more

- Occasional wobbling

- Cloudy eyes or hearing loss

This doesn't mean they're sick — just slowing down. You can help by:

- Lowering food and water dishes

- Removing high platforms or steep ramps

- Keeping bedding soft and warm

- Making sure they still eat and drink regularly

When Health Declines

Sometimes age comes quietly. Sometimes it doesn't.

If your hamster:

- Stops eating or drinking

- Has labored breathing

- Develops noticeable lumps or bumps

- Is clearly in pain or distress

- Can't walk properly or loses control of body functions

...then it may be time to talk to your vet.

They can help you understand whether your hamster is hurting — and what you can do to keep them as comfortable as possible in their final days.

It's never an easy moment, and it's never one you have to face alone. A caring vet can walk you through what's best — for your hamster, and for you.

How to Know When It's Time

There's no single rule. But you can ask yourself:

- Can my hamster eat, drink, and move comfortably?

- Is it showing signs of distress?

- Is it hiding or refusing contact?

- Are the bad days outnumbering the good?

Trust your gut. You know your hamster better than anyone.

The End: What to Expect

Hamsters may pass away:

- Quietly in their sleep

- After a brief illness

If it happens naturally at home:

- Gently remove your hamster's body

- Wrap it in tissue or cloth

- Keep it cool until burial or cremation

- Allow yourself — and your kids — time to say goodbye

If a child is involved, let them ask questions. Don't rush the goodbye. Use simple, honest language: "They died because they were very old, and their body stopped working."

Coping With Grief

Grieving a small animal doesn't mean your sadness is small.

Hamsters are companions. They wake up when the world is asleep. They take food from your hand. They learn your scent. They trust you. Losing that bond hurts — and it should.

You may feel:

- Guilt ("Did I do enough?")

- Shock (especially if it was sudden)

- Emptiness (the cage is quiet now)

- Loneliness (especially if you live alone)

All of this is normal. Give yourself permission to grieve. Talk about it. Write about your hamster. Make a little memorial.

Cry. It's not silly — it's human.

It's okay to grieve deeply — that's how you know you gave them a good life.

Talking to Kids About Death

Keep it simple. Keep it honest. Try something like:

"Hamsters don't live very long. Ours lived a full, happy life, and now it's time to say goodbye."

Don't say the hamster "ran away" or "went to sleep." These explanations confuse kids and can make them anxious about sleep or separation.

Instead, invite them to:

- Help choose a burial spot or plant a flower

- Draw pictures or write a letter

- Tell their favorite memories

- Cry, talk, or just be quiet with you

Let them see that grief is normal — and that love doesn't disappear just because life ends.

When to Get Another Hamster

There's no right answer. Some people want another right away. Others need months.

Do it when:

- You're emotionally ready

- You're not expecting a "replacement"

- You're excited about starting fresh — not trying to fill a void

When the time comes, you'll know. And you'll be even better prepared to give your next little friend the best life possible.

Summary: Life Is Short — Make It Sweet

- Most hamsters live 2–3 years

- Signs of aging include slowing down, sleeping more, and weight loss

- Watch for signs of suffering and talk to your vet if needed

- Say goodbye with love and honesty — it matters

- Grief is real, and valid, and human

- When the time is right, it's okay to love another one

Saying goodbye is hard. But it's part of the journey.

And if you've cared well, loved deeply, and learned along the way — then you've done right by your hamster. And they've done something amazing, too:

They made a tiny, unforgettable mark on your world.

Resources 1

Hamster Care Checklist

A simple checklist to help your hamster thrive

Before Your Hamster Comes Home

☐ Cage is ready (**at least 600 sq. in. of floor space**)

☐ Deep bedding (**6–10 inches for digging and burrowing**)

☐ Solid wheel (**8" for dwarfs, 11" for Syrians — no wire wheels**)

☐ A few cozy hides and tunnels for safety

☐ Water bottle **plus** a backup bowl

☐ Good-quality hamster food mix

☐ Chew toys (**wood, cardboard, or other safe options**)

☐ Safe chinchilla sand for bathing (**not dust**)

☐ Travel carrier for bringing your hamster home

☐ Cage placed in a **quiet, draft-free spot**

Weekly To-Dos

☐ Spot clean soiled bedding (daily if needed)

☐ Top up food and water

☐ Remove uneaten fresh food after a few hours

☐ Keep an eye on behavior for anything unusual

☐ Playpen/free roam time **3–5 times per week**

☐ Swap out toys and chews for variety

Monthly Care

☐ Deep clean the cage (**only if spot cleaning isn't enough**)

☐ Replace worn-out toys or hides

☐ Trim nails (**if they're getting long**)

☐ Full health check (**weigh, check teeth, fur, and movement**)

Note: Some older guides list 450 sq. in. as acceptable, but most modern hamster care experts now recommend at least 600 sq. in. for a healthier, more enriching environment.

Resources 2

Supply Shopping Guide

How to choose what your hamster really needs — and skip what they don't.

Cage

- **Good:** Large glass tank (450+ sq. in.), DIY bin cage, bar cage with horizontal climbing space

- **Avoid:** Tiny "starter kits," colorful plastic cages, cages with tubes

Bedding

- **Good:** Paper-based bedding, aspen, hemp

- **Avoid:** Pine/cedar shavings, cotton fluff, anything scented or aromatic

Wheel

- **Good:** Solid-surface wheels — 8"+ for dwarfs, 11–12"+ for Syrians

- **Avoid:** Wire or mesh wheels, wheels with ridges

Enrichment

- **Good:** Cardboard tubes, tunnels, climbing structures, foraging toys, natural wood chews

- **Avoid:** Toys with sharp edges, poorly-made plastic toys, painted or treated wood

Food & Treats

- **Good:** Reputable hamster mix, small amounts of fresh vegetables, seeds, occasional protein (like boiled egg), fresh water daily

- **Avoid:** Sugary treats, yogurt drops, citrus, garlic, onions

Grooming & Bathing

- **Good:** Dust-free chinchilla sand for bathing

- **Avoid:** Water baths, commercial "hamster shampoo," bath powders

Resources 3

Feeding & Cleaning Log

An easy way to track your hamster's care and spot changes early

Date: _____

Daily Care:
- ☐ Water Refilled
- ☐ Food Refilled
- ☐ Fresh Food Given
- ☐ Spot Cleaning Done

Weekly (Optional):
- ☐ Weight Check

Behavior Notes:

_____

_____

Print this page, copy it into a notebook, or recreate it in a spreadsheet — whatever works for you. Even small notes can make a big difference in keeping your hamster healthy

About the Author

Evan Hartley has spent years learning what makes small pets truly thrive — and sharing that knowledge with others. He writes for everyday owners who want simple, honest advice — not marketing fluff or complicated jargon.

When he's not writing, Evan is often testing out new hamster toys, volunteering with small-pet rescues, or enjoying a quiet evening watching his own hamsters dig and build their underground empires.

His goal with the *Happy Hamster Series* is simple: to help you give your tiny friend the happiest, healthiest life possible.

Thanks for Reading

If you found this guide helpful for you and your hamster, please consider leaving a quick review on Amazon.

Your feedback helps other hamster owners find reliable information — and helps me keep creating useful guides like this one.

Coming Soon: Book 2

My First Hamster – A Fun & Easy Guide for Kids & Families

Welcoming a hamster into your family? This kid-friendly guide makes it easy — and fun.

In Book 2 of the *Happy Hamster Series*, you'll discover:

- Fun hamster facts kids will love

- A playful "My Hamster Promise" pledge and chore chart

- Simple, safe ways for kids to feed, play with, and care for their new pet

- Easy DIY projects for creating hamster toys and play spaces

- A Hamster Hero Quiz and graduation certificate

Perfect for kids and parents — everything you need to start your hamster journey together with confidence and a smile.

The Happy Hamster Series

Helping Every Hamster Have a Healthy, Happy Life

Book 1: Hamsters 101 – The Complete Beginner's Guide

Your all-in-one starter guide to hamster care — from choosing the right hamster to daily care, bonding, health basics, and understanding their behavior.

Book 2: My First Hamster – A Fun & Easy Guide for Kids & Families

An engaging, interactive guide that makes hamster care fun for kids and easy for parents.

Book 3: Happy Hamster Habitats – DIY Setup & Enrichment Guide

Step-by-step projects to turn a plain cage into a hamster wonderland.

Book 4: The Hamster Owner's Survival Guide

A troubleshooting handbook for real-world hamster problems like biting, bar-chewing, escaping, illness scares, and more.

Book 5: My Hamster Journal & Health Tracker

An interactive journal to track daily care, health checks, vet visits, and special memories of your tiny friend.

Collect them all and become a hamster care pro!

Made in United States
Orlando, FL
27 December 2025

75829327R00066